SAN ANTONIO
PORTRAIT

SAN ANTONIO PORTRAIT

PHOTOGRAPHS BY
MIKE OSBORNE

FOREWORD BY
T. R. FEHRENBACH

Ⓜ️

MAVERICK PUBLISHING COMPANY

Text copyright © 2005 by Maverick Publishing Company
Photographs copyright © 2005 by Mike Osborne

MAVERICK PUBLISHING COMPANY
P.O. Box 6355, San Antonio, Texas 78209

Library of Congress Cataloging-in-Publication Data

Osborne, Mike, 1978–
San Antonio portrait / Mike Osborne; foreword by T.R. Fehrenbach.
p. cm.
ISBN 1-893271-32-3 (alk. paper)
1. San Antonio (Tex.) – Pictorial works. I. Fehrenbach, T. R. II. Title.
F394.S21143083 2004
976.4'351064–dc22

2004013472

5 4 3 2 1

Text and captions by Lewis F. Fisher

Book and cover design by Janet C. Brooks

Image scanning by Onsight

Printed in China through Asia Pacific Offset

Frontispiece: The facade of Mission Espada.

CONTENTS

✦ FOREWORD ✦

by
T. R. Fehrenbach

From its beginnings San Antonio has been a city of contrasts, which is another way of saying cosmopolitan.

The first Europeans, the Spanish coming from the south, saw the site as an oasis in the desert, a place of cool springs, clear water and old oaks rising from the burning brasada of brush-covered plains. They planted a garrison, a village of Canary Island colonists and a series of missions along the San Antonio River.

None of these had much to do with the others; friars, settlers and soldiers did not much mix, but somehow they got along. This was to be the pattern of San Antonio's growth over the next two centuries. Each wave of new-comers brought something new, but never quite assimilated or replaced the old.

This fact created San Antonio de Bexar's uniqueness, as a future metropolis where eighteenth-century walls survived beside modern office towers and where Spanish, Mexican, French, German and Anglo-American influences and cultures met, mixed and became Americanized with none becoming completely lost.

The Spanish did not do much with the town itself. Although it became the capital of the province of Texas it remained a straggling settlement. The garrison never got around to building a real fort. However, Spanish and Canary Island settlers did plant the roots of a thriving if at first meager cattle-ranching culture in the region.

The missionaries, with support from the Crown, erected grander edifices — the mission churches — with the help of prospective converts and trained artisans from the south. Due in large part to epidemics which periodically decimated their inhabitants, the missions essentially failed in their main purpose, which was to create a docile European-style agricultural population out of the local Amerindian tribes and resettle them to form new towns throughout Texas as a buffer against the French in Louisiana. Their sites remain today as monuments to Spanish imperial dreams.

Above: Begun in 1738 and completed in 1755, the main portion of Main Plaza's parish church of San Fernando has since been replaced with a Gothic Revival structure, but the domed sanctuary at the rear remains.

6

The steeple of the original St. John's Lutheran Church rises above the rooftops
of La Villita, crossable here in the 1880s only on shaky pedestrian bridges.

San Antonio remained a frontier outpost into the nineteenth century. Spanish
regulation prevented legal commerce with Louisiana and abroad (although there was
some, as archeological artifacts attest); there were no avenues to economic growth.

San Antonio suffered during the Mexican War of Independence, when many
citizens were killed by occupying Spanish royalist troops. Battles were fought in
and around the city during the Texas Revolution, the most dramatic being the
siege of the Alamo in 1836. But large numbers of citizens were not killed as in
the earlier war, when royalists decimated rebels — only the handful in the Alamo.
In fact, San Antonio became the most fought-over city in North America in these
years. During the protracted hostilities between Mexico and the Republic of Texas,
the city in 1842 was twice occupied by invading Mexican armies. Not much material
damage was done to the town, but in the 1840s the population was reduced to
some 600, as many people loyal to Mexico departed and there was no significant
Anglo-Texan immigration. In this period, the Comanche Indians could boast that
San Antonio was "their town," and they often appeared in both peace and war.

The great change in San Antonio's fortunes began when Texas joined the
United States in 1845. The city became an important army outpost, a way station
on the route to California and entered the American economy. The end of the

Overleaf: "Whisky by the Gallon, Quart, Pint" was only one of the signs greeting
nineteenth century teamsters arriving on Military Plaza. The men could count
on plenty of fast food at the chile con carne tables. After rail service shifted the
location of this transportation hub, City Hall was built in the middle of the plaza.

Mexican War drew large numbers of immigrants to Texas. Germans were especially drawn to San Antonio, as were lesser numbers of French, Poles, Czechs, Irish, Belgians.

The French influence was cultural and subtle, since France sent no masses of emigrants to San Antonio. Following Texan independence, the Roman Catholic Church in Mexico had no interest in the republic or state, where it enjoyed no enforced tithes or other privileges. The Pope assigned the region to various French orders. The early Catholic bishops were French, as was most of the priesthood until the 1870s, when jurisdiction passed to the American church. Education in San Antonio and Texas was then entirely private, the assessment of taxes to support education being held unconstitutional. French clergy gave a great boost to local schooling.

Nuns born in France opened the Ursuline Academy for girls in 1851; French brothers in 1852 established St. Mary's Institute for boys, a school that in the future fathered both Central Catholic High School and St. Mary's University. The Ursuline, which trained girls in religion and the classics for generations, was designed largely by Francois Giraud, city engineer and sometime mayor. Giraud also surveyed the city's first public park, at San Pedro Springs, where Sam Houston spoke against Secession in 1860. French architects combined excellent taste with native materials, and created monuments that were both beautiful and South-western in spirit, with a touch of French elegance.

Military aviation arrived in San Antonio — and Texas — in 1911, when Lt. Benjamin Foulois learned to fly through correspondence with the Wright brothers and took this Wright Model 1909-A aloft at Fort Sam Houston.

The Spanish tradition of fiestas remains gloriously alive in San Antonio.
Here the annual Battle of Flowers Parade celebrating Texas independence
threads past the Alamo during Fiesta Week in April 1937.

German influence was felt more in business and commerce, with mercantile
houses, banks and hotels such as the Menger, where Robert E. Lee kept a room.
So many Germans set up shop that German became the predominant language
on the streets. But the Germans built in current Southwestern or Victorian
modes. In fact, the only purely European architecture in San Antonio was found
in churches: St. Joseph's (Catholic), St. John's (Lutheran) and the Gothic towers
on the new San Fernando Cathedral, which incorporated the Spanish sanctuary
of 1738.

Much of this architecture has survived, reflecting the amalgam of Americans,
Europeans and Mexicans into an old Spanish frontier town, and it still gives San
Antonio an oddly cosmopolitan appearance for a city deep in the heart of Texas.

More important though less visual is the ambiance this amalgam produced.
The various groups — Americans, Hispanics, Germans — did not mix much in
the early days. Each lived in its own part of town. Mexicans lived on much as
before. Germans, who shocked Anglos by bringing wives and children to beer
halls, remained clannish in their societies and clubs. Anglo-Americans, who
already had a significant presence but arrived in swarms with the advent of
the railroad in 1877 and soon became the majority, kept busy with business.

11

San Antonio's modern history began in 1968, when the newly reenergized city threw a world's fair — HemisFair '68 — to celebrate its 250th birthday. Thrusting above the fairgrounds is the nearly-completed Tower of the Americas. The domed arena to its right has since been replaced by expansion of the adjacent convention center, also new in 1968. The circular building across the grounds to its left was the United States Pavilion, since turned into a federal courthouse.

However, the leading men in a now-developing city dealt with each other daily, and had to organize an effective politics and government out of disparate ethnicities. They did so, but without any one group completely assimilating the others within an Americanizing process that still goes on. This created a remarkably tolerant city, in but not entirely of its region. Southern Protestants, Hispanic and French Catholics and Germans from many different old-country areas never quite adopted each other's ways, while being subtly influenced by them.

Nor did San Antonio's newfound rail links with the rest of the nation immediately alter the familiar workings of economic, social and political activity. A boom may have sent the city's population soaring beyond 100,000 in the early twentieth century, as newly popular Spanish Colonial Revival architecture kept a familiar Southwestern flavor on grand new homes and high-rise office buildings. But San Antonio's relative geographic isolation and lack of natural resources left it mainly a mercantile, financial and military center for a broad area of Texas and Mexico, without the industry-driven dynamism that brought the huge accumulations of capital and rapid change then common to large cities elsewhere in the nation.

It was only after San Antonio threw its 250th birthday party in 1968 in the form of a world's fair — HemisFair '68 — that entrenched patterns of interaction began to change. As San Antonio's population passed the one million mark, the city's geographic center was moving ever farther north of the old downtown business district, new air travel patterns and interstate highways had ended the old geographic isolation, conventions were flocking to San Antonio and the River Walk began vying with the Alamo as the top tourist destination. A strong historic preservation movement was saving San Antonio's architectural and cultural legacies, and the long cosmopolitan history of easy tolerance was helping minority groups achieve a major role in economic development and political activity.

San Antonio has emerged as an old town growing vastly beyond its ancient plazas to the new glass towers and myriad suburban neighborhoods across its hills, but never quite losing its sense of time and place. In 1860 visitors found it remarkable that many elected officials were foreign-born, including the mayor. This ambiance of contrasts, old and new, is still alive and well in San Antonio.

13

Glass office towers rising above walls of ancient stone are, from left, the
Bank of America Building, Weston Centre and One Riverwalk Place.

◆ 1 ◆
THE SPIRIT
OF SPAIN AND MEXICO

"San Antonio is a city of the olden time, jostled and crowded by modern enterprise," thought Richard Everett. "Walking about the city and its environs, you may well fancy yourself in some strange land. The narrow streets, the stout

old walls which seem determined not to crumble away, the aqueducts — everything, in the Mexican quarter of the city especially, bespeaks a condition widely different from what you are accustomed to in any American town."

These words were penned by Everett in 1858 as he passed through with

a mule train bound for Arizona, but they seem almost as true today. San Antonio still appears "widely different" from other American cities. Waves of immigrants over the past nearly three centuries have indeed left "strange" marks — German beer gardens, French architecture, Czech pastries.

Permeating San Antonio even more, however, is the legacy of those who first settled San Antonio as an outpost on the northern frontier of New Spain, and whose kin have come from south of the border in successive waves of immigration. Language, food, love of color, a festive spirit, all these gifts from Spain and Mexico lend San Antonio even still the sense of being in another place and in a different time.

15

Above: A young San Antonio charro, a horseman in traditional Mexican dress.

Facing page: Spanish language favorites are staples of San Antonio's mariachis, including these two at Mi Tierra Restaurant.

Charros – skilled horsemen and
horsewomen in traditional Mexican
costumes – gather each Fiesta for a
charreada, a Mexican-style rodeo
reflecting horsemanship brought
by Spaniards to Mexico and Texas.

Traditional Mexican dances in the outdoor Arneson River Theater are a feature of Fiesta Noche del Rio, a twice-weekly summertime event sponsored by the Alamo Kiwanis Club.

At no time is the spirit inherited from Spain and Mexico more evident than at A Night in Old San Antonio. The annual Fiesta event, sponsored in historic La Villita by the San Antonio Conservation Society, features the food and fun of the city's numerous cultural groups. Some volunteers work at the dozens of food booths, others sell *cascarones*, confetti-filled eggshells to crack over unsuspecting victims, as some 100,000 revelers celebrate over the course of four successive April nights.

Casandra Meyer
Miss San Antonio USA

Steph
Miss

T. GEORGE
ISCOPAL

Only in San Antonio can a German singing group member, top left, take a break while leaning against a model of France's Eiffel Tower on a float in an American river parade's forming area. The Monday night parade, lower left, an annual Fiesta event since 1941, often includes a barge with the U.S. Army's Old Guard Fife and Drum Corps, based in Washington, D.C. Synthetic flowers and drapes have long since replaced real flowers for floats, top two above right, in the Friday afternoon Battle of Flowers Parade, first held in 1891. When business is slow, a vendor, below right, can sample his own *paraiso*, a frozen fruit juice bar popular in Mexico.

A San Antonio Academy cadet stands at attention near the Alamo during Fiesta. The annual celebration is held during the week that includes April 21, the anniversary of the Texans' 1836 victory at San Jacinto that vindicated the death of revolutionaries at the Alamo.

One of the finest examples of Mexican tile work in San Antonio is on the monumental archway built by Dr. Aureliano Urrutia, one of thousands of Mexicans who fled to the city during the Mexican Revolution that began in 1910. The tiles, including those in the detail on the facing page, were imported from Puebla, Mexico in the 1920s. The arch has been moved from the former grounds of his San Antonio estate to the San Antonio Museum of Art.

URUTTIA ARCH, CA. 1925; COLLECTION OF THE SAN ANTONIO MUSEUM OF ART

23

Indigenous artwork, like this in the Las Palmas neighborhood, colors the yards of many descendants of Mexican Revolution refugees who settled on San Antonio's west side.

Facing page: The Virgin of Guadalupe, patron saint of Mexico, is portrayed on a mock candle near the Guadalupe Cultural Center west of downtown.

You needn't venture closer to the border than San Antonio's downtown Mexican Market for plaster piggy banks and other wares imported from Mexico.

A spicy exterior reflects the flavor of menus at San Antonio's Mexican food restaurants.

The Torch of Friendship in the traffic circle at Commerce and South Alamo streets was donated primarily by Mexican businessmen living in San Antonio. It was designed by the Mexican sculptor known as Sebastián. In the background is the San Antonio Marriott Rivercenter Hotel, at 42 stories the city's tallest building.

A physical presence sponsored by the government of Mexico
is HemisFair Plaza's Instituto de Mexico, with exhibit rooms
and an auditorium for cultural presentations.

Defining San Antonio's role as a cultural bridge, "The Confluence of Civilizations in the Americas" was chosen as the theme of HemisFair, the 1968 world's fair symbolized by the Tower of the Americas, designed by Ford, Powell and Carson, in the background. On the facade of what has been since named the Lila Cockrell Theater, Mexican muralist Juan O'Gorman designed for Hemis-Fair a vast mosaic depicting nothing less than the history of the world. That's Adam and Eve in the center.

◆ 2 ◆
SPANISH MISSIONS
SET A STYLE

Spanish-style doorways, towers and domes came to San Antonio early in the eighteenth century with the establishment of five Spanish missions, the largest such grouping in the present-day United States. The church of the first mission, founded at the same time as the city in 1718 and now known as the Alamo, is

owned by the state of Texas and operated as a shrine to its Texan martyrs by the Daughters of the Republic of Texas. The others form San Antonio Missions National Historical Park.

Even as they fell into ruin, the missions remained a popular destination for San Antonians and other visitors. This appreciation made San Antonio fertile ground for Mission Revival architecture, which came into vogue at the beginning of the twentieth century. A Texas substyle called Alamo Revival keyed off the shape of the upper facade of the Alamo church.

Spanish Colonial Revival had superseded Mission Revival by the 1920s when San Antonio, the largest city in the largest state, was in the midst of a construction boom. It quickly became a dominant choice for residential, commercial and public buildings. Many of them are among the city's best-loved landmarks, and still help define the face of San Antonio.

Above: The style of entryways and gates like those at Mission San Juan foreshadowed similar designs in latter day San Antonio structures.

Facing page: San José Mission's sacristy window, long known as the Rose Window, is considered one of the finest examples of Spanish Colonial sculpture in the Americas.

The church of Mission San Antonio de Valero, now known as the Alamo, was begun in the 1750s but never completed. It gained its distinctive gabled parapet a century later to screen the peak of the roof put on by the U.S. Army, which used the Alamo as a supply depot before and after the Civil War.

At Mission San José, as at other San Antonio missions, walls were built as protection from raiding Apaches and Comanches. At the base of the church tower a sample has been reconstructed to show the designs that once covered the mission church exterior.

The church of San José, known
as the Queen of the Missions,
was begun in 1768, and is noted
for its Baroque exterior sculpture.

An intricately-carved doorway, completed about 1777 and shown on the facing page, opens to the sacristy adjoining the San José church. Above is the interior of the mission granary, built in the 1750s and restored in the 1930s by the San Antonio Conservation Society. Constructed, like other mission buildings, by Native Americans under the supervision of priests and of artisans trained in what is now Mexico, it once held as many as 4,000 bushels of corn.

Mission Concepción, like missions San Juan and Espada, was founded in East Texas and moved to San Antonio in 1731. Concepción has the nation's oldest unreconstructed Spanish church. Its unusual entrance features a stone triangle representing the Holy Trinity, and above it a circular window symbolizing the eye of God.

41

Above the altar in Concepción's church hangs a
painting of the Immaculate Conception believed
to have hung in the church in its earliest days.

Restoration in Mission Concepción's convento revealed a
ceiling fresco of a mestizo face combining European features
with Native American symbols of water, sun and earth.

Mission San Juan's chapel on the west side of the mission's
plaza is entered through a doorway in a partly-closed side arch.

44

Mission Espada's chapel, with its open belfry and unusual broken
arch line around the entry, was intended to become the sacristy
of an adjoining church, which was never completed.

The 1730s stone aqueduct that carries irrigation water over Piedras Creek to
the fields near Mission Espada is the oldest such structure in the United States.

While the missions served Native American converts, San Antonio's civilian community was served by the parish church of San Fernando, begun on Main Plaza in 1738. The original dome and stone walls of the altar area were saved in the larger building, begun in 1868.

During a restoration completed in 2003, an eighteenth-century-style golden
retablo was made in Mexico City and placed in San Fernando Cathedral's
original altar area. It is the approximate size of the original retablo, lost in
a fire in 1828, according to evidence found during restoration.

The building now known as the Spanish Governor's
Palace *(facing page, above)* was built on Military Plaza as
the residence of the commander of the Spanish garrison.
The keystone above the entrance *(facing page, below)* bears
the date 1749. Restoration of the building, including the
dining area *(above)*, was completed in 1931.

Mission Revival architecture was spread from California by railroad companies as the style for grand new stations. In Texas it was often modified with the familiar form of the Alamo's gabled parapet, as for the San Antonio station (1907) of the International and Great Northern, later the Missouri Pacific. The station, with its signature copper Indian atop the cupola, has been restored as the main office of City Employees Credit Union.

The federal government provided San Antonio with the state's largest planned grouping of Spanish Colonial Revival buildings with construction of Randolph Air Force Base, completed in 1930. The tower of its headquarters building, known as the Taj Mahal, screens a water tank. As is the case with so many of San Antonio's Spanish Colonial Revival buildings, it was designed by the father–son architectural team of Atlee B. and Robert M. Ayres.

Spanish Colonial Revival was the style picked by city fathers in 1926 for Municipal Auditorium, which doubled as a convention center. Colorful tiles cover the domes and provide bold patterns on the floor of the entry area. Architects were Atlee B. and Robert M. Ayres, George Willis and E. T. Jackson.

The date on the cornerstone of San Antonio's Spanish Colonial Revival city hall reveals the building's earlier origins. In 1927, the ornate Second Empire building's clock tower and corner turret roofs were removed for addition of a fourth story, as the building was remodeled by Adams and Adams in the by then more popular style.

53

Overleaf: One of San Antonio's grandest Spanish Colonial Revival homes was designed in 1928 by Atlee B. and Robert M. Ayres, with much input from its owner, Mrs. Marion Koogler McNay, then Mrs. Marion Atkinson. After her death in 1950 it became the McNay Art Museum, the first museum of modern art in Texas.

Built in 1927 on Belknap Place, in what is now the Monte Vista National Historic District, Temple Beth-El's whitewashed stucco exterior and its ornamentation reflect Spanish Colonial Revival influence. Architects were Seutter and Simons.

Perhaps the most ornate Spanish Baroque design on any of the city's commercial buildings is
I. R. Timlin's on the Auditorium Circle structure built in 1931 for Southwestern Bell Telephone.

• 3 •
A HISTORIC CITYSCAPE

Before air travel and interstate highways brought easy access to the rest of the nation and the world, San Antonio's relative isolation allowed its appearance to evolve in ways uncommon elsewhere.

Without a railroad, building materials could not be easily imported. Since large amounts of lumber were not readily available, native limestone became a  builders' favorite. Homespun architecture yielded a polyglot appearance that Frederick Law Olmsted famously described in the mid-nineteenth century as "an antiquated foreignness."

Once the railroad finally arrived in the late nineteenth century, new types of stone and brick as well as iron and steel could be brought in at competitive prices to meet the rapid growth that followed. Large panes of glass were no longer at risk of breaking while on wagon hauls overland from coastal ports. The face of San Antonio began to change.

Now-cherished landmarks were replacing older structures at an increasingly rapid rate through the 1920s, until the Depression brought new construction to an abrupt halt. Major growth resumed after HemisFair '68, forty years later. Relatively little was torn down in the interim, and even "newer" buildings had become historic. By the 1970s, preservationists were organized, tax breaks encouraged adaptive reuse and San Antonio has ended up with a unique mix of historic landmarks and picturesque neighborhoods.

Above: The bell for the new St. Mark's Episcopal Church was cast in 1876 from a cannon found buried at the Samuel A. Maverick home near the Alamo. Its inscription reads, in part, "Born again from works of death to works of life."

Facing page: The exuberant Romanesque Revival was in style when the Bexar County Courthouse was built of native Texas granite and sandstone in the 1890s.

A complex of buildings built in the 1850s and 60s for the Ursuline Academy is now part of the Southwest School of Art and Craft campus. Designers were the French-born Jules Poinsard and Francois Giraud, son of French immigrants.

A fashionable Gothic Revival facade begun in 1868 and designed by
Francois Giraud graces Main Plaza's San Fernando Cathedral, which
incorporates much of the apse of the earlier church, completed in 1749.

Trail drivers who moved cattle northward from San Antonio are memorialized in this bronze cast of part of a model by onetime San Antonian Gutzon Borglum, designer of Mount Rushmore. The full-size sculpture was intended for Auditorium Circle but was never cast. This and a companion cast flank the entrance to Pioneer Hall, north of the Witte Museum.

This typical modest San Antonio adobe home of the 1850s now stands west of the Spanish Governor's Palace. It was rented at its original location in 1894–95 by William Sydney Porter, who wrote under the name O. Henry.

The first section of the Menger Hotel was
built in 1859 on Alamo Plaza, away from older
hotels on the noisier Main and Military plazas.
Its architect was John Fries, also credited with
the distinctive front gabled parapet atop the
nearby Alamo. The hotel's original lobby
(facing page) has been elegantly restored.

Fort Sam Houston's largest individual home is Staff Post's Commanding General's home, above, designed by the English-born San Antonio architect Alfred Giles. It was renamed the Pershing House in honor of Gen. John J. Pershing, who was living there at the time he was named to command Allied forces in World War I.

Fort Sam's clock tower, left, went up in 1876 in the middle of the Quadrangle, originally a quartermaster enclosure, that has hosted deer and fowl for more than a century. Quadrangle buildings house Fifth United States Army headquarters. The post is the Army's center for medical training.

Brick barracks of the onetime Cavalry and Light Artillery Post line one of Fort Sam Houston's parade grounds. They were built at the start of the twentieth century, as the military presence in San Antonio expanded.

A decade later work began on Kelly Field. Hangar 9, left, was built on a part of Kelly Field renamed Brooks Field and, after World War II, Brooks Air Force Base. Now the privatized Brooks City-Base, it is the home of the U.S. Air Force's School of Aerospace Medicine. Hangar 9 is the only frame World War I airplane hangar surviving in the United States.

Electric lights were a novelty when San Antonio's Southern Pacific Railroad passenger station was built in 1903. They were relit when the building was restored in 1999 as part of the Sunset Station entertainment complex.

German immigrant Carl Hilmar Guenther moved his mill from Fredericksburg in 1859 to the banks of the San Antonio River at the end of King William Street, where C. H. Guenther & Son Inc. has become the nation's oldest continuously-operated, family-owned milling company.

The distinctive polychromed arches of the Kalteyer House, designed in 1892 by James Riely Gordon, help make it among the finest homes on King William Street, one of the great Victorian neighborhoods in Texas. The detail at left is from an iron fence at the Carl Groos House up the street.

The fineness of the interior woodwork at the Steves Homestead on King William Street owes much to the business of its builder, Edward Steves, a lumber magnate. Designed in 1875 by Alfred Giles, the home is a museum owned by the San Antonio Conservation Society.

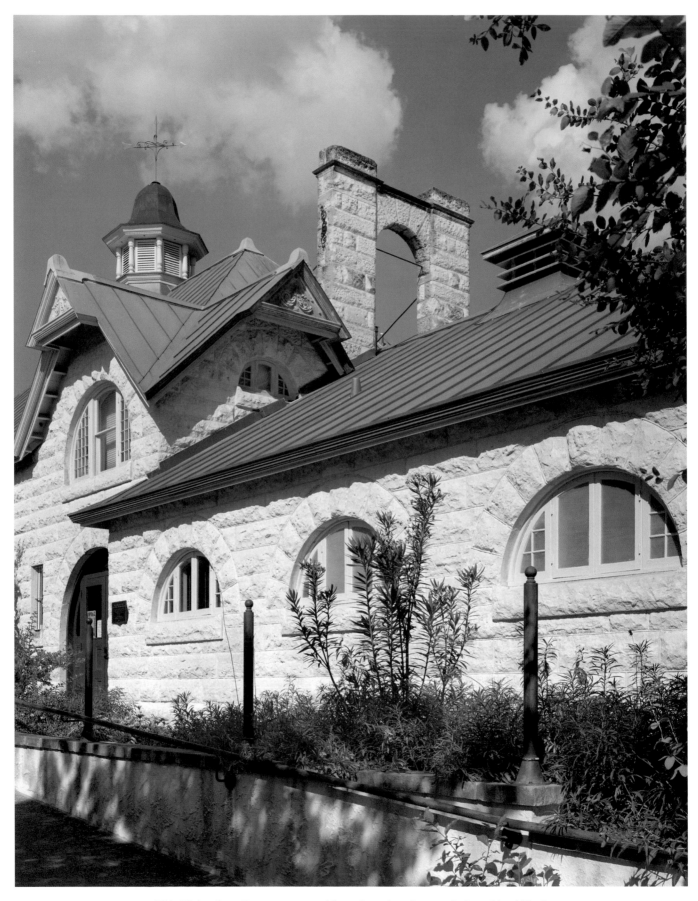

This Richardson Romanesque stable and carriage house, designed by Alfred Giles for banker Daniel Sullivan in 1896, was relocated and reassembled in 1988 as the entrance building for the San Antonio Botanical Garden.

The griffin at top guards a Queen Anne-style home built on Belknap Place in 1890. As what is now the Monte Vista National Historic District evolved, The Bushnell was built a dozen blocks away in 1926. The 7-story apartment building features elaborate detailing, below.

Well into the twentieth century, baccalaureate degrees in San Antonio were granted only by three Catholic institutions. Trumpeting angels adorn the corners of F. B. Gaenslen's chapel tower, left, at the University of the Incarnate Word. The St. Mary's University administration building, below, designed by James Wahrenberger, features components divided symmetrically into threes. On the facing page, stained glass windows designed in Germany filter daylight into the soaring English Gothic interior of Our Lady of the Lake University's chapel, designed by Leo M. J. Dielmann, while a traditional outdoor grotto stands nearby.

75

The Monastery of Our Lady of Charity, built on South Grimes Street
in 1898, has been renovated for offices of various city agencies.

The "Polish Gothic" Shrine of the Black Madonna was erected on
Beethoven Avenue by San Antonio's Polish community in 1966
to mark the one thousandth anniversary of Christianity in Poland.

Most vintage commercial facades on the south side of Commerce Street downtown were removed for widening of the street in 1912–14. Those on the north side were spared, including these, some of which date to the 1860s.

The Clifford Building, designed in 1891
by James Riely Gordon with elegant stone
detailing, rises beside the San Antonio
River at Commerce Street.

Commerce Street was home to six banks within a few blocks and was known as the "Wall Street of San Antonio" when the 22-story Alamo National Bank went up in 1929. These classic doors, designed with the structure by the Chicago firm of Graham, Anderson, Probst & White, convey a sense of unswerving dependability.

By the early decades of the twentieth century, Houston Street was replacing Commerce Street as downtown's primary thoroughfare. Keeping up with the times was the Hertzberg Jewelry Company, which moved its clock, a Commerce Street landmark since 1878, with the store to Houston Street in 1910. Both the store and its "new" building are gone, but the cast iron clock, its ownership transferred to the San Antonio Conservation Society, still tells the time.

The Buckhorn Saloon and Museum, a relic of San Antonio's Old West days, was originally located downtown and then at the old Lone Star Brewery. The brewery closed about the time Houston Street was undergoing major renewal, and the Buckhorn was reborn in a renovated Houston Street storefront.

83

The 3,000-seat Texas Theater became a Spanish Colonial Revival landmark
on Houston Street in 1926. It soon hosted the world premier of the Academy
Award-winning *Wings*, filmed in San Antonio. Its facade was preserved when
the rest of the building was replaced by a high-rise office building in 1982.

Facing page: Two landmark Houston Street theaters survive the Texas.
On downtown's western edge, Spanish language films were shown
for the Mexican-American community in the Alameda, done by N.
Strauss Nayfach in an Art Moderne design. John Eberson included a
fanciful outdoor ticket booth in his design for the Majestic in 1929.

The octagonal 30-story Tower Life Building, its ornate elevator lobby shown on the facing page, has been a major feature of San Antonio's skyline since its construction in 1928. Designed by Atlee B. and Robert M. Ayres, it was the tallest building in the city for sixty years, until displaced by the Marriott Rivercenter Hotel.

The 1927 Casino Club Building with its silvered tiered dome is a Mayan Revival landmark. It now houses retail and residential units beside the River Walk.

The corner turret of the Emily Morgan Hotel rises over both Houston Street and the Alamo, off camera to the right. It was designed by Ralph H. Cameron as the Medical Arts Building in 1926.

On Alamo Plaza, Texas heroes are sculpted in relief on a cenotaph, an empty monument honoring the dead whose bodies are elsewhere. The cenotaph, designed by Pompeo Coppini, was dedicated in 1940.

The United States Post Office and Courthouse, designed by Ralph H. Cameron with Philadelphia architect Paul Philippe Cret, has added a distinctive Neoclassical note to Alamo Plaza since its opening in 1937.

◆ 4 ◆
A CHANGING CITY

San Antonio seems to change without changing. The continually colorful mix of old and new and a persistent cosmopolitan flair make it one of the nation's top travel destinations. Two San Antonio sights — the Alamo and the River Walk, one of the world's great linear parks — vie for the title of favorite destination in Texas.

Tourists and convention-goers keep downtown vibrant, and support new theme parks and resort hotels dotting the edge of town. Though the military

presence remains important, growth of the convention industry and conversion of the former Kelly Air Force Base into a major industrial park known as Kelly USA are helping shift the city away from its traditional dependence on a service based economy. Industrial growth is also aided by construction of a Toyota assembly plant. Growth in such other areas as medicine and research are supported by rapid expansion of higher education facilities.

Increasing numbers of the million-plus San Antonians live in new suburban neighborhoods expanding ever-farther northward into the foothills of the Texas Hill Country. That may be miles from San Antonio's historic center, where the city's traditional spirit is most visibly expressed. But as crowded freeways into downtown during Fiesta week show, even the most far-flung residents can be drawn by the magnetic appeal of San Antonio's diverse heritage, and can take time to celebrate.

Above: Rivercenter Mall was built in 1988 on an extension of the San Antonio River Walk.

Facing page: North Star Mall may have Saks Fifth Avenue and Macy's, but shoppers are reminded that they are not on the East Coast by this sculpture designed by Bob Wade outside the mall on Loop 410.

93

San Antonio stretches into the Texas twilight, as seen looking
northwest from HemisFair's Tower of the Americas.

Facing page: The River Walk is transformed each Christmas
by lights hung from towering cypress trees lining the
banks. In the background is the Hilton Palacio del Rio
Hotel, at lower right Casa Rio, established in 1946
and the oldest restaurant on the River Walk.

96

A multi-level park links Main Plaza with a section of the San Antonio River
previously inaccessible to pedestrians. Known as Portal San Fernando, the
park was designed by Lake Flato Architects and completed in 2001.
Above, San Fernando Cathedral, seen through the trees at left center,
is beside the Main Plaza Building, built as Frost National Bank in 1922.

Pedestrians navigate the flagstones as water cascades through a section of the River Walk downstream from the Hugman Bridge and the Watermark and La Mansion del Rio hotels.

Informal River Walk dining settings, with pedestrians walking by, include those at Boudro's *(facing page)* and at Casa Rio *(above)*, where mariachis also entertain, briefly, a boatload of passersby.

New River Walk development outside the more heavily-traveled
Great Bend includes the Valencia Hotel and its Acenar Restaurant
(facing page), on Houston Street across from the former Texas
Theater, and, farther upstream, the stairstep waterfall *(above)* at
the Weston Centre on Pecan Street.

A new link up from the River Walk at North Presa Street makes it easier to reach the revitalized Houston Street's restaurants, shops and condominiums. One condominium complex, right, on the side not facing Houston Street still displays the fading name of a departed fashion retailer.

Rivercenter Mall's glass-lined corridors at the Commerce Street level overlook a River Walk extension.

Four high-rise buildings document the evolution of downtown development, from left: the Milam Building (1928), Crowne Plaza Hotel (1957), Weston Centre (1991) and International Bank of Commerce (1983).

"Enchilada red" is the color of the Central Library, one of San Antonio's most dramatic new landmarks. Completed in 1995 and designed by Mexican architect Ricardo Legorreta, its atrium, lower right, features Fiesta Tower, a 26-foot glass work of 917 parts by Dale Chihuly.

Corporate headquarters of Clear Channel Communications is in a Texas vernacular style designed by Overland Partners, with sleek sections of native stone and sun screens to help control direct light and heat.

109

San Antonio's Convention Center expansion, designed by Kell Muñoz Architects, includes this facade facing the Tower of the Americas on HemisFair Plaza.

The Spurs, two-time National Basketball Association champions, play at
the SBC Center, built east of downtown in 2002 and funded in part by
the San Antonio-based corporate giant once known as Southwestern Bell.

Carver Academy, a private school targeting underprivileged
Afro-American children, was designed by Lake Flato Architects
and endowed by former Spurs superstar David Robinson.

Arching tubular steel trusses provide a dramatic sense of space at San Antonio International Airport's Terminal One, designed by Heery/Marmon Mok/Simpson in 1984.

Alamo Quarry Mall preserves the chimneys of a former cement quarry operation and the renovated framework of its main processing building in a retail complex between International Airport and downtown San Antonio.

New construction continues at Kelly USA, an industrial park owned by a city-sponsored corporation since 1997. Title was conveyed to the city from Kelly Air Force Base, then the Air Force's oldest continually operating flying base, where Charles Lindbergh got his wings. Adjacent Lackland Air Force Base remains the Air Force's center for training newly enlisted recruits.

A soaring glass-and-steel entrance greets visitors to Seaworld San Antonio,
along with Fiesta Texas one of two major theme parks on the city's outskirts.

The H–E–B Science Treehouse, designed by Lake Flato Architects, overlooks the San Antonio River behind the Witte Memorial Museum's main building in Brackenridge Park.

Limestone cliffs left by a quarry in the northern section of Brackenridge Park now help enclose animals in the San Antonio Zoo, above. In a nearby corner of the park, above right, is the 1930s pedestrian arcade created by Dionicio Rodriguez, the master craftsman's prolific tinted concrete work on steel frames is, at first glance, hard to distinguish from actual wood. Much of the park is circled by a miniature train called the Brackenridge Eagle, right.

The San Antonio Museum of Art, built in 1904 as a St. Louis-based brewery, was once described as being "done up with turrets and battlements the way Mad King Ludwig of Bavaria might have done it, had he been a St. Louis beer brewer." Two wings have been added to each tower since the building opened as a museum in 1981. To the left of the west tower, shown above, is the new Lenora and Walter F. Brown Asian Art Wing. Adjoining the east tower is the Nelson A. Rockefeller Center for Latin American Art.

Facing page: A motorized sculpture moves gently above a pond near other outdoor works on the south lawn of the McNay Art Museum.

HORIZONTAL COLUMNS OF FIVE SQUARES ECCENTRIC II, GEORGE RICKEY, COLLECTION OF McNAY ART MUSEUM

Trinity University's campus on the site of a rock quarry overlooking downtown
San Antonio was designed to resemble an Italian hill town, dominated by a cathedral
— Margarite B. Parker Chapel *(above)* — and its bell tower — T. Frank Murchison
Tower *(facing page)*. These two structures were designed in the mid-1960s as a joint
venture by O'Neil Ford and Associates and Bartlett Cocke and Associates.

123

A *sombrilla*, designed by
Ford, Powell and Carson in the
1970s, shades the central plaza
of the University of Texas at
San Antonio's main campus in
far northwestern San Antonio.

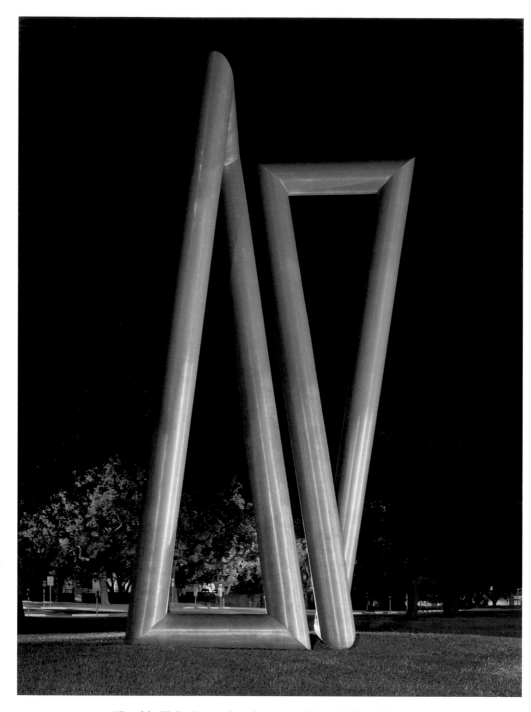

"Double Helix," a steel sculpture by Richard Harrell Rogers
representing the structure of DNA, is a focal point of the
South Texas Medical Center in northwestern San Antonio.

Tropical and desert environments are housed within the glass cones and pyramids of the San Antonio Botanical Garden's conservatory. Italian-born architect Emilio Ambasz designed the conservatory with an earthen berm around its base to help insulate the complex from the heat of Texas summers.

125

Overleaf: In this city of contrasts, fireworks set off at historic Fort Sam Houston rise above the Botanical Garden's ultramodern conservatory as part of yet another San Antonio Fiesta celebration.

◆ Acknowledgments ◆

I would like to thank Lewis F. Fisher and Maverick Publishing for the opportunity to undertake this project. Mr. Fisher's contributions to the site selection, editing and sequencing processes were invaluable. I would also like to thank Mary Ann Osborne, Gene Vogt, John Osborne, C. K. Osborne, Bill Fisher, Maverick Fisher and the rest of my friends and family who have supported my ambitions over the years.

— Mike Osborne

Especially useful information for the text was provided by Chris Carson and William McDonald, eds., *A Guide to San Antonio Architecture* (San Antonio: The San Antonio Chapter of the American Institute of Architects, 1986).